THE
IRISH
WOMEN'S
QUOTATION BOOK

GW00400044

THE
IRISH
WOMEN'S
QUOTATION BOOK

Compiled by Jane Russell

SOMERVILLE PRESS

Somerville Press Ltd,
Dromore, Bantry, Co. Cork, Ireland

©Jane Russell 2015

First published 2015

Designed by Jane Stark
Typeset in Minion Pro
seamistgraphics@gmail.com

ISBN: 978 0 9927364 3 9

Printed and bound in Spain
by GraphyCems, Villatuerta, Navarra

Front cover photo: Maude Gonne McBride
George Grantham Bain Collection,
United States Library of Congress

INTRODUCTION

The Irish Women's Quotation Book is a selection of quotations from prominent Irish women from Saint Bridget up to the present day. There is no particular theme to the book, as it incorporates politicians, suffragettes, actresses, nuns, journalists, singers and philanthropists. However, as it is very much my personal collection, the main field of activity of the women I have included is writing.

ALL THINGS BRIGHT AND BEAUTIFUL,

ALL CREATURES GREAT AND SMALL,

ALL THINGS WISE AND WONDERFUL,

THE LORD GOD MADE THEM ALL.

Mrs Cecil Alexander

Freedom

FOR OUR NATION AND

THE COMPLETE REMOVAL OF

ALL DISABILITIES TO OUR SEX

WILL BE OUR BATTLE-CRY.

Bean na h-Éireann

I HAD A
VERY HAPPY CHILDHOOD,
WHICH IS UNSUITABLE
IF YOU ARE GOING TO BE
AN IRISH WRITER.

Maeve Binchy

I WAS VERY PLEASED,
OBVIOUSLY, TO HAVE
OUTSOLD GREAT WRITERS.
BUT I'M NOT INSANE—
I REALIZE THAT I AM
A POPULAR WRITER
WHO PEOPLE BUY
TO TAKE ON VACATION.

Maeve Binchy

BECAUSE I SAW MY PARENTS

RELAXING IN ARMCHAIRS

AND READING AND LIKING IT,

I THOUGH IT WAS A PEACEFUL

GROWN-UP THING TO DO,

AND I STILL THINK THAT.

Maeve Binchy

LOVE MATCHES ARE
THOSE MADE BY PEOPLE
WHO ARE CONTENT,
FOR A MONTH OF HONEY,
TO CONDEMN THEMSELVES
TO A LIFE OF VINEGAR.

Marguerite, Countess of Blessington

PREJUDICES
ARE THE CHAINS
FORGED BY IGNORANCE
TO KEEP MEN APART.

Marguerite, Countess of Blessington

SUPERSTITION IS ONLY THE FEAR OF BELIEF, WHILE RELIGION IS THE CONFIDENCE.

Marguerite, Countess of Blessington

I COULD WISH
THAT THE ENGLISH
KEPT HISTORY
IN MIND MORE,
THAT THE IRISH
KEPT IT IN MIND LESS.

Elizabeth Bowen

ENGLAND AND IRELAND

EACH TURNED TO THE OTHER

A CLOSED, HARSH, DISTORTED FACE

—A FACE THAT, IN EACH CASE,

THEIR LOVERS

WOULD HARDLY KNOW.

BOWEN'S COURT (1942)

Elizabeth Bowen

IF YOU LOOK AT LIFE ONE WAY, THERE IS ALWAYS CAUSE FOR ALARM.

Elizabeth Bowen

WHERE WOULD THE IRISH BE WITHOUT SOMEONE TO BE IRISH AT?

THE HOUSE IN PARIS (1935)

Elizabeth Bowen

CONTENTMENT WAS
MORE NOURISHING
THAN JOY.
BEING IN LOVE
WAS NOT VERY PEACEFUL.

HOLY PICTURES (1983)

Clare Boylan

THE PEOPLE OF THIS COUNTRY

ARE FULL OF KINDNESS,

BUT ALWAYS TO STRANGERS.

WHEN A RELATIONSHIP IS REQUIRED—

LANDLADY, MOTHER, HUSBAND, WIFE,

COMPLICATIONS ARISE.

THEY DO NOT HAVE

THE FACILITY FOR INTIMACY.

BLACK BABY (1988)

Clare Boylan

I WOULD LIKE

AN ABUNDANCE OF PEACE,

I WOULD LIKE

FULL VESSELS OF CHARITY,

I WOULD LIKE

RICH TREASURES OF MERCY,

I WOULD LIKE

CHEERFULNESS TO PRESIDE OVER.

Saint Bridget

ALTHOUGH THE MAIDS
WERE THANKFUL FOR HOLY DAYS
AND WENT TO MASS,
THEY WERE REALLY MORE INTERESTED
IN AN OLD IRISH WORLD
WHERE FAIRIES, WITCHES AND
BANSHEES TOOK THE PLACE OF
OUR ANGELS AND SAINTS.
THE FARM BY LOCH GUR (1937)

Mary Carbery

THE SHY PERSON'S REVENGE ON THE WORLD.

[About acting.]

Sinéad Cusack

SOMETIMES BAD LAWS HAVE TO BE BROKEN.

Clare Daly

THANK GOD,
THO' I AM A CRIPPLE
MY MIND IS FREE
AND MY SPIRIT GOOD.

Lady Arabella Denny

ONE AMERICAN SAID THAT
THE MOST INTERESTING THING
ABOUT HOLY IRELAND
WAS THAT ITS PEOPLE
HATE EACH OTHER
IN THE NAME OF JESUS CHRIST.
AND THEY DO!

Bernadette Devlin

THE VALUE OF
UNSPOKEN THOUGHT IS LOST.
I THINK THE QUALITIES
OF HONESTY AND INTEGRITY
AND LOYALTY
WERE ALMOST LOST,
AND I VALUE THEM HUGELY.
I LOVE PEOPLE
WHO CAN KEEP A SECRET.
IRISH TIMES 11 OCTOBER 2014

Moya Doherty

And often in those grand old woods

I'll sit and shut my eyes

And my heart will wander back to

the place where Mary lies

And I think I'll see that little stile

where we sat side by side

In the springing corn

and the bright May morn

when first you were my bride.

'Lament of the Irish Emigrant'

Helen, Lady Dufferin

I HAVE A GREAT FANCY
TO SEE MY OWN FUNERAL
BEFORE I DIE.

•

OUR IRISH BLUNDERS
ARE NEVER
BLUNDERS OF THE HEART.

Maria Edgeworth

SURELY IT IS
MORE GENEROUS
TO FORGIVE
AND REMEMBER
THAN TO FORGIVE
AND FORGET.

Maria Edgeworth

IN THESE DAYS OF
COMPUTER VIRUSES,
ASKING IF YOU CAN PUT YOUR
DISC INTO SOMEONE'S COMPUTER
IS THE TECHNOLOGICAL
EQUIVALENT OF UNSAFE SEX.
INDEPENDENT 9 JANUARY 1995

Ruth Dudley Edwards

People say,
'Aren't the Irish wonderful.
So many marvellous writers.
Such a beautiful place.'
Blah, blah, blah.
No one bothers to talk about
how poverty just wears you out.
How poverty is a really
stressful, shaming tradition.

Anne Enright

SOMETIMES BEING IRISH
FEELS LIKE A JOB
YOU NEVER APPLIED FOR.
I DON'T MIND BEING IRISH,
BUT I AM NOT
A BIG FAN OF NATIONALISM.

Anne Enright

I DON'T LIKE THIS
EXCLUSION OF WOMEN
FROM THE NATIONAL FIGHT,
AND THEY SHOULD
HAVE TO WORK THROUGH
BACK-DOOR INFLUENCE
TO GET THINGS DONE.

Maud Gonne

THE ENGLISH MAY
BATTER US TO PIECES,
BUT THEY WILL
NEVER SUCCEED IN
BREAKING OUR SPIRIT.

Maud Gonne

I FEEL MORE AND MORE
THE TIME WASTED
THAT IS NOT
SPENT IN IRELAND.

Lady Gregory

IT'S A GOOD THING
TO BE ABLE TO TAKE
YOUR MONEY IN YOUR HAND
AND TO THINK NO MORE OF IT
WHEN IT SLIPS AWAY FROM YOU
THAN YOU WOULD WITH
A TROUT THAT WOULD
SLIP BACK INTO THE STREAM.

Lady Gregory

THE ITEMIZED PHONE BILL
RANKS UP THERE WITH
SUSPENDER BELTS,
SKY SPORTS CHANNELS
AND *LOADED* MAGAZINE
AS INVENTIONS WOMEN
COULD DO WITHOUT.

MAIL ON SUNDAY 25 APRIL 1999

Maeve Haran

THERE IS AN IRISH WAY OF
PAYING COMPLIMENTS
AS THOUGH THEY WERE
IRRESISTIBLE TRUTHS,
WHICH MAKES WHAT
WOULD OTHERWISE
BE AN IMPERTINENCE,
DELIGHTFUL.

Kathleen Tynan Hinkson

THERE ARE MANY FORMS
OF CENSORSHIP, AND FROM
PERSONAL EXPERIENCE,
I KNOW THAT SELF-CENSORSHIP
BY JOURNALISTS OF WHAT
THEY WRITE AND REPORT,
IS THE MOST CORROSIVE.

Mary Holland

IF AN IRISH ARTIST OF THE
EIGHTH OR NINTH CENTURY
WERE TO MEET
A PRESENT-DAY CUBIST OR
NON-REPRESENTATIONAL PAINTER,
THEY WOULD UNDERSTAND
ONE ANOTHER.

Mainie Jellett

I ALWAYS WONDER WHY
PEOPLE TALK ABOUT GUILT
IN THE CATHOLIC CHURCH.
IT'S SHAME.
WOMEN ARE TAUGHT SHAME.

•

THINGS ARE STILL EASIER FOR MEN,
JUST AS THEY ALWAYS HAVE BEEN.

Dilly Keane

IRELAND IS
THE LAST BASTION
OF CIVILIZATION.

Molly Keane

As a writer, I'm always insecure. It's not exactly that I'm waiting for rejection but you just never know.

Cathy Kelly

IT HAS BEEN SAID THAT
TIME HEALS ALL WOUNDS.
I DON'T AGREE.
THE WOUNDS REMAIN.
IN TIME, THE MIND,
PROTECTING ITS SANITY,
COVERS THEM WITH SCAR TISSUE,
AND THE PAIN LESSENS,
BUT IT IS NEVER GONE.

Rose Kennedy

GRATITUDE IS AN ATTITUDE,
NOT A FEELING.
MOMENTS OF STILLNESS (2009)

•

JOY IS A GIFT.
SEARCH FOR IT AND
YOU WON'T FIND IT.
PRAY FOR IT AND
IT WILL COME TO YOU.
GARDENING THE SOUL (2001)

Sister Stanislaus Kennedy

Nurturing a grudge can be
a full-time occupation.
Unspoken anger does not
bring us freedom,
but instead keeps us
locked to the other person.
The glue of unresolved
resentment keeps us
stuck in silent pain.

Gardening the Soul (2001)

Sister Stanislaus Kennedy

I WAS DRAWN TO FEMINISM
AS A YOUNG WOMAN BECAUSE IT
WAS THEN CALLED
'WOMEN'S LIBERATION'.
IT WAS ABOUT FREEDOM.
TODAY IT IS ABOUT EQUALITY.
FREEDOM MEANS DIFFERENCES
ALWAYS EMERGE: EQUALITY MEANS
FREEDOM WILL BE CURTAILED.

Mary Kenny

I'VE TRIED TO OBSERVE MY
MOTHER'S ADVICE
ABOUT MARRIAGE:
'NEVER LET THE SUN GO DOWN
ON YOUR ANGER; AND NEVER
GIVE A MAN BAD NEWS ON AN
EMPTY STOMACH'.

Mary Kenny

AT 69, I DYED
MY HAIR PURPLE
AND ACQUIRED A TATTOO.
YOU HAVE TO KEEP DOING
NEW THINGS AND
DIFFERENT THINGS
FOR AS LONG AS YOU LIVE.

Mary Kenny

ONLY A BLOCKHEAD SAYS
'JE NE REGRETTE RIEN'.
REGRETS ARE PART OF THE
EXPERIENCE OF THOUGHT AND
REFLECTION, OF LEARNING AND
CORRECTING, OF DRAWING
LESSONS FROM FAILURE,
AND OF THE STRANGE, BITTERSWEET
SENTIMENT OF RUEFULNESS.

Mary Kenny

I'D RATHER
DIG A DITCH THAN
GO TO A DINNER PARTY
WITH PEOPLE
I DON'T KNOW.

Marian Keyes

MY TRUTH IS THAT
WHAT DOESN'T KILL YOU
MAKES YOU WEAKER
RATHER THAN STRONGER,
ALTHOUGH IT
MAKES YOU WISER.

Marian Keyes

I'VE ALWAYS BEEN
MELANCHOLIC.
AT A PARTY,
EVERYONE WOULD BE
LOOKING AT THE
GLITTERING CHANDELIERS,
AND I'D BE LOOKING AT THE
WAITRESS'S CRACKED SHOES.

Marian Keyes

TAKE UP CAR MAINTENANCE
AND FIND THAT THE CLASS
IS FULL OF OTHER THIRTY-
SOMETHING WOMEN
LOOKING FOR A FELLA.

LAST CHANCE SALOON (1999)

Marian Keyes

MY HEART WAS NATURALLY GOOD...BUT THE NATURAL GOOD WAS FREQUENTLY PERVERTED BY EVIL EXAMPLES.

Margaret Leeson

We are a vibrant
first world country but
we have a humbling
third world memory.

Mary MacAleese

CHILD ABUSE REVELATIONS
GREATLY AFFECTED PEOPLE'S
VIEW OF THE CHURCH.
EVERYTHING YOU THOUGHT
YOU HAD, EVERYTHING YOU
THOUGHT YOU WERE,
BECAME A LIE.

Mary MacAleese

WHAT IS
MORALLY WRONG
CAN NEVER BE
POLITICALLY RIGHT.

Mary Anne McCracken

I WILL NEVER ACCEPT THE KING OF ENGLAND AS THE KING OF IRELAND.

Mary MacSwiney

A STRONG TIDE OF LIBERTY SEEMS
TO BE COMING TOWARDS US,
SWELLING AND GROWING
AND CARRYING BEFORE IT
ALL THE OUTPOSTS THAT
HOLD WOMEN ENSLAVED AND
BEARING THEM TRIUMPHANTLY
INTO THE LIFE OF THE NATION
TO WHICH THEY BELONG.

Countess Markievicz

We have to get rid of
the last vestige
of the Harem
before woman is free
as our dream of the
future would have her.

Countess Markievicz

Fix your mind on the
ideal of Ireland free,
with her women enjoying
the full rights of
citizenship in
their own nation.

Countess Markievicz

I AM AMBITIOUS, YET THE STRONGEST POINT OF MY AMBITION IS TO BE EVERY INCH A WOMAN.

Lady Sydney Morgan

All our failures are ultimately failures in love.

The Bell (1958)

Iris Murdoch

ONE OF THE SECRETS OF A HAPPY LIFE IS CONTINUOUS SMALL TREATS.

THE SEA, THE SEA (1978)

Iris Murdoch

ONE DOESN'T HAVE TO GET
ANYWHERE IN A MARRIAGE.
IT'S NOT A PUBLIC CONVEYANCE.
A SEVERED HEAD (1961)

•

THE CRY OF EQUALITY PULLS
EVERYONE DOWN.
OBSERVER SEPTEMBER 1987

Iris Murdoch

I THINK BEING A WOMAN
IS A BIT LIKE BEING IRISH.
EVERYONE SAYS YOU'RE
IMPORTANT AND NICE,
BUT YOU TAKE SECOND BEST
ALL THE SAME.

Iris Murdoch

HUMILITY IS NOT
A PECULIAR HABIT OF
SELF-EFFACEMENT,
RATHER LIKE HAVING
AN INAUDIBLE VOICE,
IT IS A SELFLESS RESPECT
FOR REALITY AND ONE OF THE
MOST DIFFICULT AND CENTRAL
OF ALL THE VIRTUES.

THE SOVEREIGNTY OF GOOD (1970)

Iris Murdoch

WE LIVE IN
A FANTASY WORLD, A
WORLD OF ILLUSION.
THE GREAT TASK IN LIFE
IS TO FIND REALITY.

THE TIMES APRIL 1983

Iris Murdoch

THE 1916 MYTH,
LIKE MALARIA,
IS IN MY BLOODSTREAM.

A PLACE APART (1978)

Dervla Murphy

WE TALK ABOUT ABORTION
AND THERE'S AN UPROAR.
BUT WHAT ABOUT THE
BILLIONS OF CHILDREN
THAT ARE ALREADY
OUT THERE?

Christina Noble

GETTING OLDER IS GREAT, YOU LEARN TO LET STUFF GO, LIKE YOURSELF.

The Nualas

THERE'S NO DISAGREEMENT THAT CAN'T BE SOLVED WITH A GOOD CUP OF TEA, IN THE FACE.

The Nualas

THE VOTE
MEANS NOTHING
TO WOMEN.
WE SHOULD
BE ARMED.

Edna O'Brien

I'M AN IRISH CATHOLIC AND I HAVE A LONG ICEBERG OF GUILT.

Edna O'Brien

I HAVE SOME
WOMEN FRIENDS
BUT I PREFER MEN.
DON'T TRUST WOMEN.
THERE IS BUILT-IN
COMPETITION
BETWEEN WOMEN.

Edna O'Brien

MY MOTHER ALWAYS SAID
IF THE PROTESTANTS
CATCH A CATHOLIC
IN THEIR CHURCH
THEY FEED THEM
TO THE JEWS.

Kate O'Brien

EVERYWHERE I GO,
I'M ASKED IF I THINK
THAT UNIVERSITY
STIFLES WRITERS.
MY OPINION IS THAT
THEY DON'T STIFLE
ENOUGH OF THEM.

Kate O'Brien

GOD HAS
THE MOST WICKED
SENSE OF HUMOUR.

•

ABOVE ALL,
DEEP IN MY SOUL,
I'M A TOUGH IRISHWOMAN.

Maureen O'Hara

I WAS ELECTED BY THE
WOMEN OF IRELAND,
WHO INSTEAD OF
ROCKING THE CRADLE,
ROCKED THE SYSTEM.

Mary Robinson

THERE ARE MANY STRANGE THINGS
BEYOND OUR KNOWLEDGE,
AND MAYBE THERE
ARE GHOSTS TOO,
THOUGH I DO NOT UNDERSTAND
WHY THEY SHOULD
COME BACK TO THIS WORLD
WHEN THEY HAVE GONE FROM IT.

Peig Sayers

HAD I KNOWN IN ADVANCE
HALF, OR EVEN ONE THIRD,
OF WHAT THE FUTURE
HAD IN STORE FOR ME,
MY HEART WOULDN'T
HAVE BEEN AS GAY OR
COURAGEOUS AS IT WAS
IN THE BEGINNING
OF MY DAYS.

Peig Sayers

IF CURSES COME
FROM THE HEART,
IT WOULD BE A SIN.
BUT IF IT IS FROM THE LIPS
THEY COME, AND WE USE THEM
ONLY TO GIVE FORCE
TO OUR SPEECH, THEY ARE A
GREAT RELIEF TO THE HEART.

Peig Sayers

To be honest I live among the English and have always found them honest in their business dealings. They are noble, hard-working and anxious to do the right thing. But joy eludes them, they lack the joy that the Irish have.

Fiona Shaw

THE LESSON OF
THE IRISH RISING
AND ITS SUPPRESSION
IS THAT
OUR SMALL NATION,
IRELAND,
HAS A RIGHT TO
ITS PLACE IN THE SUN.

Hanna Sheehy-Skeffington

THE IRISH AND THE ENGLISH
UNDERSTAND EACH OTHER
LIKE THE FOX AND THE HOUND.
BUT WHICH IS WHICH?
AH WELL, IF WE KNEW THAT
WE'D KNOW EVERYTHING.

EXPERIENCES OF AN IRISH RM (1899)

Edith Somerville and Martin Ross

FIRST OF ALL, THE MOST
IMPORTANT THING IS TO
LEARN EVERYTHING GOOD
THAT HAS SURVIVED
FROM OTHER TIMES AND
CAREFULLY TO WATCH THE
BAD—AND THROW IT OUT.

Ninette de Valois

IF YOU STAY,

EVEN IF YOU GO TO PRISON,

YOU WILL ALWAYS BE MY SON...

BUT IF YOU GO,

I WILL NEVER

SPEAK TO YOU AGAIN.

[Her views on Oscar Wilde fleeing
to France to avoid prosecution.]

Lady Jane Wilde

SELECT BIBLIOGRAPHY

Broderick, Madan, *Wild Irish Women* (Dublin: O'Brien Press, 2002).

Gross, John, (Editor), *New Oxford Book of Literary Anecdotes* (Oxford: OUP, 2006).

Kavanagh, P.J., *Voices in Ireland* (London: John Murray, 1994).

Keane, Molly and Phipps, Sally, (compiled by), *Molly Keane 's Ireland* (London: Harper Collins, 1993).

Kemp, Peter, (Editor), *Oxford Dictionary of Literary Quotations* (Oxford: OUP, 1997).

Knowles, Elizabeth, (Editor), *Oxford Dictionary of Quotations*, Eighth Edition (Oxford: OUP, 2014).

Quinn, John, (Editor), *A Portrait of the Artist as a Young Girl* (London: Methuen, 1987).

Randall, James, (Editor), *Bloomsbury Anthology of Quotations* (I.ondon: Bloomsbury, 2002).

Seoighe, Mainchín, (Editor), *Irish Quotation Book* (London: Robert Hale, 1992).

Sherrin, Ned, (Editor), *Oxford Dictionary of Humorous Quotations*, Second Edition (Oxford: OUP, 2001).

IRISH WOMEN INDEX